QUIRKY ESSAYS FOR QUIRKY PEOPLE

THE COMPLETE COLLECTION

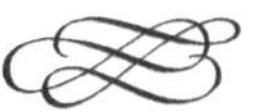

BARBARA VENKATARAMAN

CONTENTS

BOOKS BY BARBARA VENKATARAMAN

Death by Didgeridoo (Jamie Quinn Cozy Mystery #1)

The Case of the Killer Divorce (Jamie Quinn Cozy Mystery #2)

Peril in the Park (Jamie Quinn Cozy Mystery #3)

Engaged in Danger (Jamie Quinn Cozy Mystery #4)

Jeopardy in July (Jamie Quinn Cozy Mystery #5)

Malice in Miami (Jamie Quinn Cozy Mystery #6)

Jamie Quinn Mysteries Box Set: Books 1-3

Jamie Quinn Mysteries Box Set: Books 4-6

Jamie Quinn Mysteries Box Set: Books 1-6

I'm Not Talking About You, Of Course (Quirky Essays for Quirky People #1)

A Trip to the Hardware Store (Quirky Essays for Quirky People #2)

A Smidge of Crazy (Quirky Essays for Quirky People #3)

Teatime with Mrs. Grammar Person

If You'd Just Listened To Me In The First Place

The Fight for Magicallus

Accidental Activist: Justice for the Groveland Four (Co-Author)

Scary Shorts: Flash Fiction

Holiday Shorts: Flash Fiction

Valentine Shorts: Flash Fiction

Dog Days of Summer Shorts: Flash Fiction

A Year of Shorts: Flash Fiction

A TRIP TO THE HARDWARE STORE

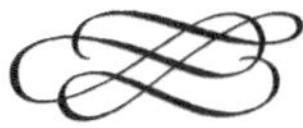

He always gave it his best when it came to home repairs, but my dad was in way over his head. The problem was that he wouldn't admit it. Whether it was a leaky faucet or a blown fuse, somehow he always made it worse. Then the experts would be called in, the plumbers and electricians, the plasterers and sprinkler repairmen. Invariably, the first thing they would say is: "Too bad you didn't call sooner, now I have to charge you double." As a result, nothing could get my Mom out of a chair faster than hearing the jangle of keys and my Dad yelling over his shoulder: "Back soon, I'm going to the hardware store." But she was always too late to stop him.

"Not the hardware store!" became a family joke over the years, one that never got old, but no amount of teasing on our part could ever convince my dad to stop trying. The truth is, he would have been happy with just *one* success, one amazing home repair that he could show off and say, with practiced nonchalance: "Oh, that? Yeah, I fixed it myself. Took me no time at all."

Like Charlie Brown, my dad kept trying to kick that football only to have the house yank it away at the last minute, just like Lucy. The most perplexing thing was my dad's crazy optimism that *this* time would be different. Failure was not an option in his mind, but it had become an expectation in ours. We braced ourselves for the worst and, sure enough, one day it arrived...

I awoke that morning to the sound of my sister yelling from inside the shower. Since the shower was just on the other side of the wall, it sounded like she was yelling right in my ear, through a megaphone. It was the worst wake-up call ever, but it turned out she had a good reason for pitching a fit. There was no hot water, not a drop! And with four teenage girls in the house, this was a crisis of epic proportions. This time, we couldn't afford to take any chances. Before my dad knew what hit him, Norman the plumber had been called in to assess the situation.

"Well," Norman said, solemn as a funeral director, "what you have here is a leaky pipe and there's no telling where it's coming from. Could be the size of a pinhole, but that's all it takes. The bottom line is--it's easy to fix, but it's a nightmare to find."

Realizing that *someone* would have to dig up the floor, (and that we couldn't afford for Norman to be that *someone*), my mom made a decision. She knew it wouldn't end well but she had no choice. Turning to my dad, she did the unthinkable. She said, "Arthur, you need to go to the hardware store."

This was his last chance to prove himself and my dad was determined to get it right. Luckily, it wasn't complicated stuff. All he had to do was dig up the floor and find the leak so Norman could fix it, then fill the hole with cement. And, if his daughters didn't suffer more than a few hours of substandard hygiene, he knew he would be a hero.

The logical place to start digging for our underground hot spring was the kitchen, where the floor felt warm under our bare feet. My mom was relieved that the leak seemed so easy to find, but I wasn't convinced. Didn't anyone else remember what Norman said?

Armed with a sledge hammer, my dad attacked the floor with real enthusiasm. It was back-breaking work, but he was a man on a mission. Besides, he wanted to finish in time to watch the Dolphins game that afternoon. Wet chunks of concrete were popping up from the floor like gray popcorn and my dad put his glasses on to protect his eyes. The *bam bam bam* of the sledge hammer was giving me a headache and I had more important things to do, like talk on the phone, and fight with my sisters over the phone, so I went to my room. (Hey kids, in the "old" days, we only had one phone and the six of us had to share it!)

When my dad finally reached the pipe a couple of hours later, we heard him groan. Actually he cursed, but this is a "G" rated story. And, no surprise, the leak wasn't there. Water was flowing INTO the kitchen from somewhere beneath the dining room. My mom started to look concerned about the carpeting. One thing was for sure-- my dad was going to miss the first half of the game.

We were recruited to move the dining room furniture. The only thing we left was the light fixture, hanging in the middle of the room. Under my mom's supervision, my dad gently pulled up the carpeting and padding then continued his path of destruction into the dining room. Thankfully, there was nothing else we could do--except feel sorry for our poor dad. By this time, he had taken off his shirt and sweat was pouring off him. I mean, he hadn't done that much exercise since--well, as long as I'd known him. And certainly not since then either.

Anyway, he kept digging and digging (not really digging, more like smashing) until the entire dining room was a construction site. To give you an idea, there was a giant hole in the floor shaped like Florida: the panhandle was in the kitchen, St. Augustine was near the laundry room and the Keys were starting to encroach into the living room. My dad was so exhausted he was struggling just to lift the sledge hammer. As he hoisted the hammer off the ground and swung it high over his head, we watched in horror as he smashed the overhead light fixture into a million pieces! Showers of glass rained down, most of it lodging in my dad's back. He started bleeding from at least a dozen different places. The room looked like a crime scene! We all rushed to his aid and, after cleaning and bandaging his wounds, we called Norman in for a consultation. Sure enough, Norman spotted the leak through all the debris and mucky water and repaired it in no time.

That hiatus allowed my dad to lick his wounds (I mean that figuratively), replenish his fluids and get dressed because he had to go back to the hardware store (which I assume was no longer his favorite place). I don't know how many bags of cement he had to lug home, but it was a lot, hundreds of pounds' worth. Once he got home, he opened the sliding glass doors to the backyard, removed the screen and pulled the hose into the house so he could mix the cement in a wheelbarrow. The poor guy mixed and shoveled cement for hours. He looked like he was ready to collapse. When he had finally filled the cavernous hole to the top, he smoothed it until it looked like glass. Sorry, painful analogy, he made it as smooth as an ice skating rink after the Zamboni passed over it.

While we were congratulating my dad on his huge accomplishment, Boris (our Bassett Hound who lived outside during the day), made a break for the house. It's not Boris' fault for thinking he was invited in, the door was wide open. You guessed it, Boris ran right across the fresh cement! My dad unleashed all of his pent-up frustration yelling at Boris to get out and poor Boris became so flustered he peed all over the wet cement. My dad had to redo the whole floor.

In the end, we had a funny story, my dad had a project he could be proud of, and my mom never heard about the hardware store again.

DINNER IS SERVED

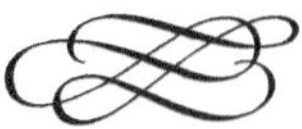

I'D BEEN THINKING ABOUT IT FOR MONTHS, HOW great it would be for all my friends to get to know each other. Then the pieces of my life would fit together like a jigsaw puzzle, or a Dickens novel where all the good, well-intentioned people wind up together at the end. And so I made a plan: I would invite them all to dinner and cook something fabulous. I don't like to brag, but I do have some specialties. Besides, with two cable channels offering cooking shows 24 hours a day, who could ever run out of recipes? I figured that after we polished off a few bottles of wine and a gourmet dinner, new friendships were practically guaranteed.

It took some finagling since we are all busy women, but after dozens of e-mails and texts we finally picked a date. Husbands were put on alert, babysitters were booked, and children were given ultimatums. I had a dinner to plan!

I wanted to start with my favorite salad: romaine lettuce, bleu cheese crumbles, cranberries, candied walnuts and a sesame dressing, but then I remembered: Mai is allergic to sesame and Joette is allergic to walnuts. Unless I wanted to serve Benadryl chasers with the wine and EpiPens as a second course, the salad had to go. Maybe something simpler would work-lettuce, tomatoes, and cucumbers? But no, with Leslie's diverticulitis, she couldn't eat anything with seeds or she'd end up in the hospital for a week...Good thing I remembered!

I decided to give up on salad altogether. Instead, I would serve a crudité platter with carrots and celery and a curry dressing. Done! Wait-not so fast, the curry dressing calls for milk and Monika is lactose-intolerant. Isn't there a brand of lactose-free milk now? Whew! Crisis averted.

For the main dish, I planned to make Macadamia-nut encrusted chicken in orange sauce. Everyone always loves that (especially me) and it's foolproof. Also, it can feed a crowd. Then I realized the sweet orange sauce could cause problems for my diabetic friend. Hmmm...I guess I could omit the orange juice. But what about the vegetarians? There were a couple of those in the group, so I decided to substitute soy nuggets for the chicken. Problem solved. And it could've been worse, they could've been vegans. Or PETA people. Nothing against PETA, but I had no place to stash my leather sofa.

Moving on to the side dish, I wanted to make a yummy casserole that is just to die for. It's called "Soubise," which is French for start licking your lips now. It's made with rice and loads of buttery, sautéed onions (*two pounds* to be exact) and some grated Swiss cheese. Then it is baked to fluffy perfection. Oh rats! My friend Judy can't eat onions, they give her acid reflux. I would have to leave them out.

By the time I started thinking about dessert, I was feeling rather stressed, but I figured if I stayed away from strawberries (because of the seeds) and walnuts, I should be okay. That is, I wouldn't end up killing any of my guests.

The big night arrived and we gathered in my cozy little house. It suddenly occurred to me that maybe this was a bad idea, maybe these women wouldn't like each other at all. I felt like success or failure was riding on me, but I needn't have worried. My wonderful friends were their wonderful selves and by the time we sat down to eat, they had bonded like sisters.

I had worked really hard on my dinner party and wanted it to go well. While I was hoping for a flawless evening, I was willing to settle for a memorable one. And I got my wish. After my guests admired the culinary masterpieces on their plates, they reached for their forks and took a bite. Had they actually been sisters, they couldn't have looked more alike at that moment because they all wore the same stunned expression.

How could food so lovingly prepared taste this awful?

I'll tell you how--by not following the recipes! After I explained the minefield of dietary issues I'd had to navigate, we had a good laugh and decided to order pizza. As I dialed the pizza parlor, this is what I heard:

"No onions on mine, please."

"I need one without cheese..."

"I can't digest peppers because of the seeds."

"Mushrooms make me gag."

"If there's meat anywhere on the pizza, I won't eat it..."

As it turns out, they really were sisters.

LAZY BONES

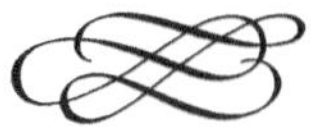

EFFICIENT PEOPLE ARE REALLY LAZY PEOPLE IN disguise--true or false? If you said false, you clearly aren't one of us. The truth is we lazies strive to do as little as possible as quickly as possible so we can get back to lazing around. Being efficient fits nicely with our goals and, more importantly, it gets better press.

Case in point: a quick peek at the dictionary reveals that "efficient" means being productive with minimal effort, while "lazy" means requiring little or no effort. See? They're the same. Except, of course, for the synonyms. Oy! If you're lazy, you are *indolent, shiftless and slothful.* Slothful! When the best way to describe you is by invoking the Seven Deadly Sins, you know you're in trouble. On the other hand, if you're efficient, Mr. Roget and his eponymous book can't praise you highly enough. Not only are you energetic and economical, you are also capable and clever, able and accomplished, shrewd and skillful, and also, my personal favorite, *virtuous.*

Not to mention that lazy is often followed by the word "bastard."

So unfair. And where's the gratitude? Where would the rest of you be if *we* hadn't perfected procrastination? Take Hamlet, the biggest procrastinator of all time...okay, not a good example. What you need to know is this: procrastinating is an art. A person can dabble in it for years and never become a virtuoso. Only a master procrastinator can leap from the precipice of putting things off into the whitewater of wasted time to swim in the sea of snide remarks without drowning.

Isn't it time the world lauded our contributions to society? Look at our magnificent "Paper Self-Management System" which enables offices everywhere to run smoothly. Also known as "Elimination by Procrastination," this system allows the user to dispose of piles of paperwork without ever touching them. The secret lies in recognizing which documents will take care of themselves without human intervention. It also works with e-mails, texts and voicemails.

Another of our crackerjack accomplishments is "National Procrastination Week." Troubled by the stressful lives of our friends and neighbors, we wanted to show them an easier life--our life, and so we instituted "National Procrastination Week"

(March 4th-10th), to promote the many benefits of putting off until tomorrow everything that needn't be done today. You're welcome.

Of course, I would be remiss if I didn't introduce you to some famous procrastinators in history. First, we have President Woodrow Wilson who prohibited child labor, limited railway workers to an eight hour day, declared war on Germany and wrote fourteen points about something or other. I should probably look that up. I'll do it later, I need a snack first ... oops, where was I? Oh yes, the important thing was Wilson's firm belief that: "Today's greatest labor-saving device is tomorrow."

And then there's Mark Twain, father of American literature and the greatest humorist of his age. He was one of ours. Did you know he changed his name to Mark Twain because it took too darn long to write Samuel Langhorne Clemens? Think of all the time he saved over a lifetime! He even patented several time-saving devices including an "Improvement in Adjustable and Detachable Straps for Garments" (to replace suspenders) and a self-pasting scrapbook featuring pages coated with dried adhesive that only required moistening. Genius!

And talk about efficient, when Twain learned that his birth coincided with the appearance of Halley's Comet, he declared that he would die when it returned. And, of course, he did. His motto was:

"Never put off until tomorrow what you can do the day after tomorrow."

Our third American hero is Les Waas, founder and president of the "Procrastination Club of America." The club boasts 12,000 active members and millions more who are planning to join, but haven't gotten around to it. The club started as a joke when Waas and some friends hung a sign up in a hotel that read: "The procrastination's club meeting has been postponed." Waas has been president for fifty-five years and explains that while the club would like to award an annual "Procrastinator of the Year," they are still waiting for the nominating committee to make a recommendation. (Steel, Piers, Ph.D. The Procrastination Equation. New York: Harper 2010).

So, what are the roots of procrastination? Is this just a modern-day reaction to our perpetual busyness? Excellent questions, glad you asked. Some ancient civilizations did embrace the concept of procrastination. Indian philosophy, for example, gives equal weight to the paths of action and inaction, and one of the foundations of Zen Buddhism is to live in the moment, aware of your actions, thoughts and sensory perceptions.

Hey multi-taskers! Turn off your phones and pay attention. You don't see any Buddhist monks racing around town picking up their dry cleaning and dropping their dog off at the vet, do you? That's because they're serene. They're living in the moment. They're in tune with their inner selves. Nah, they're probably just procrastinating...

The bottom line is: don't feel guilty for procrastinating. The important stuff will get done eventually and the other stuff will take care of itself. It turns out some of the most creative people are the biggest procrastinators. Virginia Woolf wrote in *A Room of One's Own:* "It is in our idleness, in our dreams, that the submerged truth sometimes comes to the top." See? You weren't procrastinating, you were just being creative!

YOUR ACCOUNT IS PAST DUE

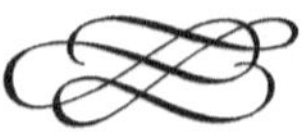

IT WAS BOUND TO HAPPEN, BUT STILL, IT WAS embarrassing. When you send out as many collection letters as I do, eventually, you'll send one to a friend or acquaintance without realizing it. Oops! Major faux pas...

When people find out I do collection work, they usually give me a look that says, *Oh, you're one of them.* Then they remark that it must be *so unpleasant* to do that sort of work. I pretend to agree because I can't tell them the truth--I enjoy it. And why not? I can make a living chatting with people, listening to their stories, and making deals with them, all from the comfort of home. Usually in my pajamas. Just kidding, I get dressed sometimes. Like on laundry day...

Bill-collecting is a lot like coaching little league: some days, you have to explain the rules, other days, you have to break up a fight or give a pep talk, but it's all good. And like little leaguers, my people have a hazy sense of time, especially when it comes to making a payment plan. Even when the present looks bleak, they're convinced the future will be rosy. They are eternal optimists--but I know better. Although I don't have a crystal ball, I'm pretty sure their lives won't be any different in six months. Except that things could get worse...

I shouldn't give away all my secrets, but my method of bill-collecting requires me to eat a sandwich as part of the process. Allow me to explain. Let's say, someone makes an offer to settle a debt. No matter how good the offer is, I can't accept it without breaking my number one rule which is: *never take the first offer*. Not even if it's for payment in full. Just kidding, I'm a stickler for the rules, but I'm not crazy.

My second rule of collection is to...always...pause at...critical moments in... the negotiation. People hate uncomfortable silences so much that they rush to fill the void-- and wind up outbidding themselves. Without me having to say a word. After listening to their offer, I explain to them that I need to speak with my client. And *that's* when I eat a sandwich--but not while I'm talking to them, that would be rude. The fact is I already know what my clients will accept, so I don't need to call. After lunch is over, I contact the debtor to propose a higher amount, knowing that I can always take less, but this is my last chance to ask for more. And more is better, especially since I get thirty percent. (To clarify, there are times when less is more, but this is not one of them.)

The strangest part of my job is that *I never meet these people.* We talk and correspond, sometimes for years, but I can't put a face with a voice, or picture the guy with the funky handwriting. The sad truth is that I talk to my debtors more than I talk to my relatives, and it's probably the same for them. Not that my debtors are talking to my relatives--what I mean is--oh, never mind...

I can't help it if people want to tell me their life stories. Whatever their motivation is, they sure do some peculiar things, considering that I'm chasing them for money. For example, one woman texts me on every holiday just to wish me a happy holiday. Another sends me her checks wrapped in a piece of paper she signs, "Hugs, Phyllis." Still other people send me notes thanking me for my patience and understanding. *My husband claims I write these notes myself, but it's just not true. If I'd written them, I would have been much more effusive...*

Some of the stories I hear are truly unbelievable and when I say stories, I mean excuses for not paying. Some are tragic, of course, and I am sympathetic to those people. All I can do is tell my client what's going on and recommend that they write off the debt. The other stories I hear are more tragi-comic. Here are some of my favorites:

-I can't pay right now because a trailer flew across the turnpike during the last storm and slammed into my house.

-I can't pay this week because my girlfriend stabbed me and I just got out of the hospital. Also, I ran out of checks.

-You don't scare me, I've been to prison. (BTW, he *is* paying, and I didn't do anything to scare him)

And my favorite excuse of all time:

-Sorry I haven't paid, but I was in a bad accident--didn't you hear about it? My car went off the road into a canal swarming with alligators during mating season and I barely escaped! I was in the hospital so long I lost my job. Now, I've been diagnosed with PTSD and I'm also *deathly* afraid of alligators, but I can honestly say it was the best thing that ever happened to me. I'm so grateful to be alive! I love my life, and I love my kids and even my annoying friends don't seem so annoying anymore. I promise you I will pay this debt,

Amazingly, she did pay it off three months later, so I assume she got a job--maybe as a motivational speaker. All I know is she's my official winner, at least until someone can top *that* story...

And now I have a confession to make: I really like my debtors, even the quirky ones. Take Bill, for example. When his checks wouldn't arrive on time, and they never did, I would call him. He always knew it was me, so instead of saying "hello," he would answer the phone by saying: "I SWEAR to you, the check is in the mail." I would sigh to convey my deep disappointment and say, "Bill, you're killing me, do you know that?" Then we would both laugh and I'd get the check two days later.

Another debtor I'll never forget kept promising to pay but didn't, and eventually I gave up on him. *Two years later*, he sent me a check for the full amount with a note that said, "Here's the money I owe, sorry it took so long."

I ask you, why can't I instill that kind of guilt in my kids?

Then there was Darlene. Her husband was stationed in Iraq and she was just trying to make ends meet. Before sending a payment, she would call first and I always remembered to ask about her husband. She finished paying the debt before her husband returned. Now I'll never know if he made it home.

And poor Vinnie owed money to my friend Kay. Their kids played football together and it always made Kay mad to see him, knowing he owed her money. She didn't realize how embarrassed he was to see her because he didn't have the money to pay.

But the one who made me laugh was Mike. After making a payment plan, he had the chutzpah to ask if I would call and remind him every month.

I said, "Not unless you're planning to send me a Mother's Day card."

He only hesitated a second before answering, "Sure, I can do that."

My faux pas...I forgot about rule number three: Don't be sarcastic, it will only get you in trouble.

And I can tell you, it doesn't work with little leaguers either.

GADGET GIRL

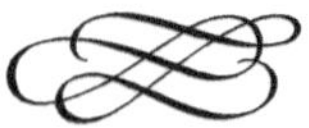

IF THE OPPOSITE OF "HOARDER" IS A PERSON WHO despises clutter, knick-knacks, gewgaws and tchotchkes, then I am that person, with one notable exception. Although I worship Minimalism as a philosophy, and also as a house-cleaning technique, I admit I have a weakness: I love gadgets–specifically, kitchen gadgets. I can't help it. While I can easily ignore the siren call of an infomercial (Seal in flavor! Juice it! Grill away fat!) and I've never purchased a Ginsu knife (who wants to cut their sneakers in half?), I just can't resist a cool gadget. Maybe it's the way they solve problems I didn't know I had, but my online dictionary got it right, a gadget really is an "ingenious device."

Let's start low-tech with the *apple slicer*. Now, tell me this: who wouldn't enjoy eating a crisp Fuji,

Gala or Granny Smith apple cut into eight perfectly symmetrical slices? Nobody, that's who. When Eve took a bite of her first apple, she had to be wondering, "Isn't there an easier way to eat this thing?" She would have appreciated the apple slicer.

Of course, if you want to bake your apple, you should put away the slicer and take out your *apple corer*. Once that pesky core is gone, you can fill your apple with yummy deliciousness like honey, raisins & cinnamon, and then top it off with vanilla ice cream when it's baked. See what you've been missing? Luckily, both of these gadgets are inexpensive and fit neatly in your kitchen drawer.

Things start to get tricky if you're a garlic-lover, and honestly, who isn't? The first gadget you'll need is a *garlic keeper* so your garlic stays fresh as a daisy, er, just fresh. Next up, you'll want to buy a *garlic roaster* because-- what's the point of eating fresh-baked, crusty bread if there's no roasted garlic to spread on it? You'll need only a few more gadgets to complete your set: a *garlic peeler*, a *garlic press*, a *garlic slicer*, a *garlic dicer* and a *magic soap bar made of stainless steel* to take away the garlic smell. Personally, I enjoy the smell of garlic. I'd like to create a garlic perfume called "Delicioso." A light spritz would make you smell like a world-class chef and, in the event of a culinary crisis, you could also spray it on your food. All of these gadgets are essential, but don't worry, they won't take up much space, only half of a kitchen drawer.

Since you still have some room in the drawer, you should consider adding these beauties: a *tomato stem remover, a corn stripper, a lemon zester, a grapefruit segmenter, an herb snipper with a stem stripper, an avocado slicer, a strawberry huller, a cherry pitter, an olive stuffer, a ravioli stamper, a calzone mold,* and my absolute favorite, an *egg-cuber,* so you can make square hard-boiled eggs that won't roll off your plate. Genius!

Now that your drawer is full, let's talk about the fun stuff. You can't live without a *Popsicle maker* if you have kids--that's a fact–and you just can't beat the smell of fresh bread wafting from your *automatic bread maker.* If you pour the ingredients in at night and set the timer, you'll be dreaming you live in a bakery as you bake fresh bread in your sleep. If you're health-conscious, then an *electric yogurt-maker* is perfect for you, and you can always beat the summer heat with your *electric ice-cream maker.* Think of the exotic flavors you could invent, like bourbon with cornflakes, or candied bacon--you can't find those in the store! And how about those fancy Paninis you can make with your *Panini Press?*

But we aren't done yet! Just think how much you'll enjoy the gentle gurgle of seltzer water flowing from your *Sodastream* and the Belgian waffles you made in your *waffle iron,* not to mention the fries you fried in your *Fry Daddy*, the coffee you ground with your *coffee grinder*, the noodles spiraling out of your *pasta maker* and the perfectly prepped lettuce leaves shooting out of your *salad spinner*. When you're done with all that, you can bathe in your *chocolate fountain*. Isn't life good?

You may be wondering where to put all of these amazing gadgets. It's simple really, just get rid of your knick-knacks, gewgaws and tchotchkes, and any other useless clutter, like dishes, pots & pans, and all the food in your pantry, and you'll have plenty of room for all this neat stuff. Enjoy!

WHERE DID THE TIME GO?

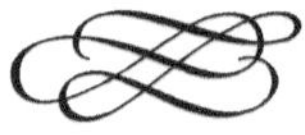

My Tuesdays have gone missing. I only looked away for a second, I swear, but when I turned around, they were gone. So now, it's good-bye to my to-do list, my second cup of coffee and the rigorous exercise program I was just about to start. I even miss my trips to the dry cleaner. Sigh...

Before you panic and hire a security guard to keep an eye on *your* Tuesdays, let me assure you, yours are perfectly safe. Mine was an inside job, and I know the thief all too well. In fact, I've known him all my life. The worst part is that he's not sorry at all. Well, he might be, if he ever figured out it was him, but probably not then either.

You see, it's my dad, and he is starting to lose it. He thinks he's just fine, which tends to complicate matters. At eighty-two, I guess he's entitled to depend on his children more, especially since he's fended for himself until now, but I can't help wishing he'd taken better care of himself along the way. Although he feels fine, he takes a pill for everything and requires the services of a dozen doctors--one for each organ, and a few more for good measure. If that weren't bad enough, each new doctor gives him multiple appointments (like multiples of five), and lab work which is always scheduled for the crack of dawn, on the other side of town.

For the two or three of you still unfamiliar with managed care, let me explain how it works: each appointment and test needs a *separate* referral from the primary doctor. These are given out only on the second day following the third night after a full moon. Also, you have to know the secret password. Got it?

And so, my missing Tuesdays are spent making appointments, begging for referrals and, of course, driving my dad all over the place, including the supermarket. Here in south Florida, you can always see elderly people at the grocery store during daylight hours. Many of them are shopping with their *middle-aged children* (an oxymoron if I ever heard one), having heated discussions about which cereal to buy and whether they really need cigarettes.

Suddenly, I am one of them...but which one? My vision blurs and I am an old lady. I'm in the cereal aisle arguing with my son. He wants me to buy Fiber

One, but I am demanding Froot Loops, why can't I have Froot Loops? Who does he think he is?

I feel myself hyperventilating and stagger over to the freezer section where I yank open the door and stick my head in the sub-zero air. Hovering above the green beans, I take deep breaths and recite a soothing mantra. My father sees nothing unusual about this and keeps walking.

Feeling calmer, I relinquish the freezer to a woman waiting patiently behind me. She gives me a nod, just as her elderly mother catches up with the cart. She knows my story because she's living it. I track down my father, who has filled the cart with groceries he doesn't need and won't use. He forgot that he eats all of his meals in the dining room of his assisted living facility. Also, he doesn't know how to cook.

Later, we grab a slice of pizza and I tell my dad a joke, which makes him laugh. I honestly can't remember if I've told him that joke before, but since he can't remember either, it works out. As we eat, I notice how much he resembles my grandmother now. At the same time, I realize that we are mirror images of each other--the way we sit, how we hold our pizza. I start to feel dizzy as the past, present, and future spin together, pulling me into a swirling vortex. I long for the cold embrace of the green bean freezer. When my father asks me if I'm alright, I tell him *Yes, I was just having a hot flash...* which isn't actually a lie.

On the drive back to my dad's assisted living facility, I can't help but notice the "Silver Alerts" flashing overhead, warning motorists that a confused old person somehow got a hold of the car keys and took off. Luckily, we took my dad's car away before that happened, but we almost didn't. My sisters and I were so naïve, we actually thought he'd ask for help if he needed it. But he knew exactly what we'd do, so he pretended everything was fine. It took us a year to realize his memory was slipping.

As I drop my dad off, I watch him greet everybody (not by name, of course) and then wander off into the bingo room. Unburdened by memory and unaware of his medical issues, he is carefree. And while he may not remember all of his grandkids' names, he knows he loves them. It's not a bad life, but still, I'm determined to hang onto my memory. I've done some research and found out that the best way to ward off dementia is to be physically active, keep your brain engaged, take complex B vitamins and consume turmeric, the bright orange spice used in curry.

So, I hope you'll excuse me now, but I have to go do some jumping jacks, finish my Sudoku puzzle, gulp down my vitamins and eat some turmeric. I think it would be perfect sprinkled over Froot Loops.

BEYOND BELIEF

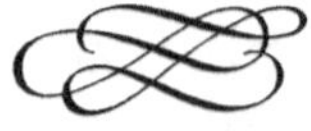

We weren't married very long when my husband brought it up.

"I can't believe you used to be a waitress."

"Why is that?" I asked, sweeping up broken glass from the kitchen floor.

"Well," he said, trying to be diplomatic, "you drop a lot of stuff."

"So, I'm a klutz," I said. "That's not news. Not grounds for an annulment either, if that's what you're thinking," I said, authoritatively. "Not in this state."

"Not a problem," he said. *But I still can't believe you were a waitress.* Now I understand why you went to law school, there was nothing you could break. Except the law, of course..."

"You're *hilarious*. Listen, I was a great waitress," I said. "Make some popcorn and I'll tell you all about it.

~

My first foray into the food industry was at McDonald's. I know--that's not waitressing and McDonald's isn't food--but, all the same, the customers were cranky, the bosses were bossy, and I reeked of French fries by the end of the day, so it counts. The most annoying thing was that Lori, my supervisor, would constantly tell me to "look busy." Apparently, I worked too fast for her. No sooner did I finish mopping then she'd tell me to re-mop the clean floor. There was just no point in discussing it. Logic was wasted on her, and humor wasn't a gene she'd been burdened with, so I just kept mopping the clean floor, and waiting on customers, of course.

Another thorny issue for Lori was *suggestive selling*, as in 'Would you like fries with that?' I hated doing it, and she hated me for not doing it. I was passive and she was aggressive, we were the Yin and Yang of McDonald's. Can you imagine me suggestive selling to my clients now? 'I'll prepare your contract right away. And would you like a lawsuit to go with that?' I mean, that would be crazy..."

~

"So, did she fire you?"

"No way! I quit, and I bet Lori cried herself to

sleep over it, too. Anyone can swing a mop, but she'll never find another sparring partner like me.

༄

My next waitressing gig was a Chinese Restaurant near my house. I don't remember the name of it and it's long gone, but there was one memorable thing about it--I was the *only* non-Asian employee. I thought I'd be the odd one out hearing Chinese spoken all around me, but I was wrong. While I was definitely an outsider, it wasn't because they were speaking Chinese, no, it was because they were speaking SPANISH and Chinese. They were all from Cuba! If you think "Spanglish" is hard to understand, try "Span-ese" (I just made that up). And the drama! Oh, they had more romance, betrayal, jealousy and intrigue going on there than in a telenovela. But I couldn't figure out any of it, and I wasn't crazy about the food either, so I left.

Which brings me to "Peoples", a chain restaurant with a gigantic salad bar and inexpensive entrees. I think there's one in Texas still, but the one in Florida didn't last long. The thing about Peoples was the food came out *fast* and I really had to hustle to keep up. One day, I was running my legs off when I got seated with yet another table, which put me totally in the weeds. I needed to take their order and then grab my food from the kitchen before the manager saw it sitting there.

Naturally, my new customers, who spoke with a southern drawl, were in no hurry at all. I was stressing out as the couple asked me a zillion questions about every item on the menu. Finally, finally, the husband, a big beefy guy, looks up and says to me, 'I'll have a quickie.' I just stood there, mouth open, pen in mid-air. The man politely said it again, 'I'd like a quickie, please.' I asked him to *point to the item on the menu*. I was afraid he would start acting it out or something. Turns out he wanted a *quiche*. Clearly, not a popular dish in his home state, if they had them at all.

At the end of that summer, I left for law school. I was dying to get to New Orleans!

Law school was the pits, but New Orleans was so amazing that I didn't mind having to work part-time. The Riverbend Restaurant was upscale, but not too fancy, and it was close to campus. Remember I had just worked at Peoples where speed was not only encouraged, but expected.

During my first week at the Riverbend, I was incredulous at how slowly food came out of the kitchen, so I hung around the cooks asking them *when* was my food coming up. Finally, Miss Adele, the manager, an older woman with big hair, ambled over to me and said, "Honey, let me tell you something. I don't know where you used to work, but our food here does not come out of a can. We cook it by hand and that takes time..." Then she smiled at me and that's the moment I became a real waitress. I still miss that place. I think it got knocked down to build a Winn Dixie...

The next summer I worked for Masa-San Japanese Restaurant, the most fun place I ever worked. It was right next to my parents' office and owned by a man named, you guessed it, Masa-San. My sister Michele and I worked the lunch shift along with a cook who was always hung-over and only spoke Japanese. Michele and I ate Japanese food for breakfast, while Masa and the cook ate doughnuts from down the street. After we made friends with the night shift waiters, we all went bowling together one night, armed only with a Japanese/English dictionary so we could communicate. I don't know what we actually said to each other, but we laughed the whole time. I heard Masa eventually moved back to Japan.

I may have been in a Japanese immersion program by day, but by night I was a cocktail waitress at Victoria Station, a restaurant cleverly constructed to look like three connecting train cars. It was cute, it was fun and it was easy, except for one thing: all of the frozen drinks were served in tall glasses so top-heavy that we worried constantly about spilling them--*especially* me.

One night, it finally happened and in the worst way imaginable. Picture a misstep, a shaky hand and a large frozen strawberry daiquiri with whipped cream toppling off a tray in slow motion, spilling right onto a bald man's head! I'll never forget the tears, the recriminations, the non-stop apologies, and the look on that poor man's face when he got slimed. What a night! I wish that place was still around so I could take you there. And the funniest thing about that daiquiri spilling was that *I wasn't the one who did it....*"

~

"I notice a theme running through your story," my husband said, as he grabbed a handful of popcorn.

"That I'm not as klutzy as you thought?" I asked, smugly.

"No--that every restaurant you ever worked for closed right after you left."

I caught him off-guard when I threw my popcorn at him, but soon it was all-out war with a snowstorm of popcorn flying through the air. Luckily, we hadn't buttered it. After I took out the broom for the second time that night, my husband asked, "Hey, do you want to go for a walk? We could use the exercise."

I kicked back in my comfy recliner. La-Z-Boys are for girls too, although they don't like to advertise it.

"Nah, I'd rather watch TV," I said, picking up the remote. "By the way, did I ever tell you I used to be an aerobics instructor?"

HIGH FINANCE

MY SISTERS AND I CALL IT "HIGH FINANCE," BUT there's nothing high-end about it and honestly, even we don't understand it. Our system is so complicated, so convoluted, that it would make a seasoned accountant switch careers-but only after he drank himself into a stupor. The fact is, there's no algorithm or mathematical formula that can explain it--it just works. And although high finance can be as elusive and ephemeral as a fleeting thought, with no logic or reason, it's always there when we need it.

While we're not exactly sure how it started, or why we keep doing it, my sisters and I wouldn't have it any other way. The truth is we enjoy it. It's a game we play with a worthy purpose, and it saves us time. Really, it does. Oh sure, it makes our husbands crazy, but that's just an added bonus. Whenever we say,

"Time for high finance," they roll their eyes, throw up their hands and try to butt in. But we're stubborn women, and quite bossy besides. If they thought they could change us, they should have married someone else.

"*Here we go again...*" says one brother-in-law.

"Why don't you pool your money or something?" suggests another.

"Good luck with that," says my husband.

"You're just whistling into the wind..." says the fourth one. He's been around the longest.

Listen guys, we know there are easier ways, but this works for us. High Finance serves as our collective memory, a link that gives us another excuse to interact--as if our kids, husbands, pets, and aging father weren't enough. We use 'telegraphese' to get the job done through e-mail, texts, phone calls and, of course, face-to-face contact.

After some haggling over the division of labor, ("Come on, I got the last three gifts!") money may change hands, but probably not. We usually hold back on payment, knowing that another event can't be far off. And future transactions could give you a credit, *or even wipe out your debt altogether*, and that is a thing of beauty.

Now, the usual gift-giving obligations are easy to handle and hardly test our formidable skills. Birthdays, anniversaries, December holidays, graduations, Father's Day--these flow like a calm river through our busy lives. And despite having to remember twenty-one birthdays, we are unflappable. It's the other life events that stymie us, the ones that pop up unexpectedly, like when we need baby gifts, get-well bouquets, congratulation cookies or funeral flowers. These make us nuts. Luckily, we know one of us will handle it and that we'll settle up eventually. In this way, we give each other the gift of time, shortening three to-do lists at once, just like that. Then we caretakers can feel taken care of for a change.

I have to admit that it can get mighty confusing at times. Here's a typical scenario. Let's pretend our names are Ella, Bella, Della and Stella.

"Stel-la!"

(Sorry, I couldn't resist, but I bet you sounded *just* like Brando when you read that. I know I did.)

Okay, here goes...

"Hey, you guys each owe me $50 for Dad's birthday," says Ella.

(B, D & S owe E $50)

"Okay, but Bella & Della each owe me $30 for Ella's kid's birthday," says Stella. (B & D owe S $30)

"I bought the platter for Uncle _______'s funeral, that was $100, and I also picked up cookies for Dad's nurses

for $40, so you guys owe me $35 each," says Della. (B, S & E owe D $35)

Bella says, "Just tell me what I owe everybody..."

And so, after all the numbers are crunched:

Stella owes Ella $50

Della owes Ella $15.00

Stella owes Della $5

Bella owes Ella $50, Stella $30 and Della $35

Stella tells Bella, "Pay what you owe me to Ella, then I owe her $15."

Della tells Bella, "Pay what you owe me to Ella, then she owes me $20."

Stella tells Della, "Just forget the $5."

And so on...

Checks fly back and forth but in the memo part we always write "Even Steven." That way we know we've caught up. And if we aren't planning to get together, we might mail the check with a note that says "Even Steven, love you!"

We come by this craziness honestly, as a legacy from our mom. She always took care of everyone, which explains why, when she died, it was standing room only at her service. Later, as we sorted through her things and found her address book, we saw phone numbers for gift basket and florist shops in every city we had ever lived in, as well as the cities where our relatives lived. So, it shouldn't surprise you to hear that we bought gift baskets for her hospice nurses...I think Stella took care of that, because Bella got the last thing.

And so, as part of my estate planning, I've decided that, along with my last will and testament, I'm going to leave each of my sisters some money with a note that says, "Even Steven. Love you!" Just in case we don't get a chance to settle up.

I'M NOT TALKING ABOUT YOU, OF COURSE…

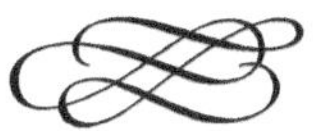

I'M NOT TALKING ABOUT YOU, OF COURSE, BUT pet owners can be so annoying. Oh, I know what you're thinking-that I just don't understand and that, clearly, I have never experienced the joy of pet ownership. To that I say you may have a point. But, seriously, why the need for a bumper sticker that proclaims: "I love my Labrador Retriever"? Are you hoping that fellow Labrador enthusiasts will feel a kinship towards you and avoid rear-ending your car? Or, are you hoping they will pull up next to you at a traffic light to chat about Labs? I don't get it...And I also don't understand people who plaster pictures of their pets all over their office (or cubicles) at work. They have dozens more pictures than I have of my kids (does that make me a bad mother? do they enjoy making me feel inferior?) And they always want to tell you stories, *lots* of stories about how brilliant, charming and adorable their pet is and why their pet should perform on the Letterman show.

Well, I need to set the record straight: I have indeed owned pets and have even lived with other people's pets. In fact, my favorite roommate in college also happened to own my least favorite cat in the world. This cat hissed and nipped at me any time I encroached on his territory, which apparently was the entire apartment with the exception of my room. I tried to win him over, but he was unimpressed. The most amazing thing was how oblivious my roommate was to her cat's open hostility. She explained that he liked me-he was just being "standoffish."

When I was a kid, my father brought home a Bassett Hound and named him Boris. He was kind of cute, in a droopy sort of way, (the dog, not my father) but, if Boris liked us, he kept it to himself. He also had one particularly unendearing quality, he smelled terrible! And no amount of bathing could change that. Naturally, my mother didn't want him in the house, except at night when he slept in the utility room-with the door tightly closed. Undaunted, my father bought Boris a dog house. If Donald Trump decided to keep an outside dog, he would buy this exact dog house. It had all of the amenities, including indoor/outdoor carpet and a fan, and it was huge! Our tree house wasn't half as nice, not that I harbor any resentment. Well, not anymore. My Dad was so proud of that dog house that he actually took people outside to take a tour.

One day, it was pouring like it would never stop. My dad looked out the window and then slammed his coffee cup down. "Unbelievable! Boris is standing out in the rain! Why doesn't he go in his dog house?" My dad marched outside and, while we watched through the window, he tried to show Boris how to go into the doghouse by crawling on all fours and going into it himself. Boris just stood there as the rain pelted him from every direction. Frustrated, my dad proceeded to half-carry, half-shove the recalcitrant hound into his palatial home. But, as soon as Boris was inside, he turned around and walked out again. After spending an hour in the rain *trying to keep the dog from getting wet*, my Dad came in the house, exhausted and soaked to the bone, muttering, "What a stupid dog..."

Soon after that, we had to give Boris away due to his other bad habit, which we didn't even know he had. One after another, our neighbors began calling to complain. It turned out that when we weren't home, Boris howled non-stop. He was so loud, he was scaring their children. They couldn't hear their TV sets even with the windows closed. So it was "Bye bye Boris," we hardly knew you.

And don't think my experience with pet ownership ended there. No Sir, it did not. When our boys were young, they convinced us that we needed a dog.

Foolishly, we decided to rescue a dog from Animal Control, not realizing that our chance of finding a normal dog there was practically zero. As it turned out, cute little Sunny was in a class by himself- a little Cock-a-Poo with a big problem. It wasn't a problem for him, it didn't faze him a bit, but when Sunny received anything more than a passing glance, he became so excited that he wet the floor. Sadly, we could only be friendly to Sunny when we were outside; inside, we had to maintain a cool cordiality from a safe distance.

We were prepared to live with Sunny's strange quirk if it hadn't been for his *other* issues. First, he started snapping at non-existent flies; then he started licking his left front paw incessantly for no apparent reason (although I'm sure he had an *excellent* reason for snapping at imaginary flies). The vet prescribed Prozac for his OCD (yes, dogs can have OCD), but it didn't help. Soon after that, Sunny started jumping up on the table and peeing on the mail (on purpose!) and he had to go.

Several peaceful, pet-free years passed and our memories faded to the point that when our youngest son begged for a dog for his birthday, we capitulated. Somehow, we ended up with not one but two dogs, sisters named Abby and Phoebe. Vivid memories of Sunny suddenly returned and we waited for the nightmare to begin again but now times two! We waited and waited and...nothing happened. Well, something happened. We discovered that we had two perfectly house-trained dogs who were sweet and good-natured and only barked at the mailman. Soon, we learned how brilliant, charming and adorable they could be and so clever that they were sure to be on the David Letterman show one day. I just happen to have some pictures, would you like to see them?

IRRATIONAL FEARS

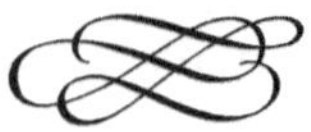

Even if you are *THE* most well-adjusted person alive today, somewhere buried deep in your psyche lives an annoying little kid who looks a lot like you and has an irrational fear of....something. Who knows how it started? Maybe you read a scary story once, or maybe you were hurt or *almost* hurt doing something, but now it is forever imprinted in your brain...to be afraid.

My own fear of lightning (Keraunophobia) is just one of my mother's many fears, handed down at a susceptible point in my childhood. I know for a fact that my mother was never struck by lightning, nor did she know anyone who even came close, but the minute she heard thunder, she tore out of the house, stopped our game of "kick the can" (even if we were winning!) and herded us into the house so fast we didn't know how we got there.

And she was "the lightning police" for the entire neighborhood. One day, the kids across the street were swimming in their above-ground pool while their parents weren't home (!) and it started thundering. With nary a thought for her own safety, my mother dashed over there and made them get out of the pool NOW. While she did not enjoy other people's misfortune, quite the contrary in fact, she still felt compelled to tell you whenever some unfortunate soul, often on a golf course or a baseball field, had been struck dead by lightning, usually *out of the clear blue sky.*

Living in Florida, the lightning capital of the country, helps to keep my fear alive and well and I'm quite sure I'll never shake that one off. I am also afraid of bears but it's only a problem when we visit a National Park where they happen to live, so that fear doesn't limit me so much. But, as I grow older, I am developing some new fears including: Catoptrophobia (fear of mirrors), Barophobia (fear of gravity) and Geniophobia (a fear of chins).

My friend's mother was afraid of riding in elevators, (a combination of acrophobia and claustrophobia) which was quite a manageable fear, and my younger son was afraid of clowns (Coulrophobia) for quite a while after seeing the movie "It." As long as he never joins the circus, he should be alright. My older son suffered from Lachanophobia (a fear of vegetables), but he is slowly outgrowing it.

I know many people who suffer from Ergophobia (a fear of work), Phronemophobia (a fear of thinking) and Gnosiophobia (a fear of knowledge), but they don't find it debilitating in the least. Thankfully, I don't know anyone who suffers from Ablutophobia (fear of washing or bathing) and I personally could never associate with people who had Hippopotomonstrosesquippedaliophobia (a fear of long words, of course).

Luckily, people with Paraskavedekatriaphobia (fear of Friday the 13th) only have to freak out three times a year, at most, and sometimes only once a year, but the ones I feel most sorry for are those who suffer from Panophobia (fear of *everything*) and Phobophobia (fear of fear). Is that what FDR meant when he said: "The only thing we have to fear is fear itself"?

Even if your particular fear doesn't have an official name, don't feel bad, I'm sure there is someone who feels the same way you do. You could probably even find a support group online, unless of course you suffer from Cyberphobia (a fear of computers) or Anthropophobia (a fear of meeting new people). Then maybe you should just go lie down until you feel better, *but don't look under the bed*, just in case.

IT ALL STARTED WITH A LOUD SNEEZE

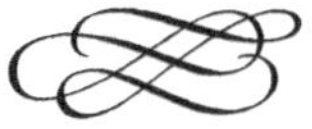

It all started with a loud sneeze. One minute I was chatting on the phone and the next I was down on all fours chanting "ow ow ow OW!" I had never thrown my back out before and I wondered if I would ever get off the floor. From this new perspective, I realized that I could now "keep my ear to the ground" *and* my "nose to the grindstone" with no effort at all. Eventually, the spasm subsided and I crawled to the bathtub to take a hot bath. A few days later, a physical therapist recommended back exercises for me. Her favorite was "wall-sitting." Wall-sitting is simply standing with your back to the wall and then bending your knees until you resemble a human chair. Then you stay that way as long as you can. She also recommended a half hour of Pilates. I vowed to wake up early every day to fit all of that in.

The next week I went to the dentist for a check-up. He told me that, at my age, I should brush twice daily, floss, use a Water Pik ® (like a pressure cleaner for your teeth) at night and then stimulate my gums with a rubber-tip between each tooth, front and back. I vowed to stay awake a half hour later every night so I could fit all of that in.

The next week I went for my annual check-up. My doctor told me that, at my age, I should be doing 30 minutes of aerobic exercise three times a week and also working out with weights to keep up my bone density. He added that if I wanted to remain flexible, I should start doing Yoga. I decided to give up my lunch hour and also wake up an hour earlier on the weekends so I could fit all of that in.

The next week, I went to the dermatologist for a check-up. She told me that, at my age, I should stay out of the sun at all costs and slather myself with sun-screen any time I saw the light of day. So I bought a case of sunscreen and vowed to spend an extra fifteen minutes getting ready every morning so I could fit that in as well.

After a month of my new routine, I was so sleep-deprived that I started combining things so I could stay in bed longer. I became the "Queen of Efficiency." I flossed my teeth while I practiced being a human chair; I rubbed sunscreen on while I jogged in place and I stimulated my gums with a rubber pick while holding a Yoga pose of a tree. Instead of lifting weights, I juggled the cans of beans as I was making dinner and carried the dog out of the kitchen. Finally, after I started doing deep knee bends while I brushed my teeth, I found I didn't have to wake up early anymore. This getting older stuff is totally manageable-I don't know why everyone complains about it. Excuse me but I feel a sneeze coming on...

A JOLT OF ELECTRICITY

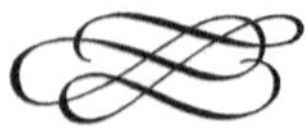

During moments of quiet reflection, I ponder deep philosophical questions, like: "If Amish people could time-travel to the past, would they notice?" If you never spend time in quiet reflection (perhaps because your TV is blaring and your cell phone is ringing), then try to imagine that you have no electricity, telephone or car. Forget about lights, that's the least of your problems. You have no washing machine, dryer, dishwasher, vacuum cleaner, television (!), computer (!) or, *gasp!*, air conditioning... Sorry, I had to stop for a minute, I was feeling faint. Like most Americans, I am so addicted to electricity that I would need a twelve-step program to wean myself off of it. I know people who are so wired to their smart phones, laptops, iPads & MP3 players that if they could open a vein and safely run electrical current through their bodies to power up, they would happily do it. Those people would never have survived the two weeks I spent living like the Amish...

It was during the hurricane season of 2005 and Hurricane Wilma had weakened from a Category Five to a Category Two before bearing down on us. The torrential rains and punishing winds cost the country billions of dollars, but, fortunately for us, our only damage was a carpet of debris in the yard. Oh, and the loss of power. Sitting in a darkened, hurricane-shuttered house without the comforting hum of electricity buzzing through your appliances is like entering a sensory deprivation chamber. Suddenly, the house that provided every creature comfort and an endless array of amusements has become anathema to you; *you must escape, but there is nowhere to go except*-OUTSIDE. The nurturing womb you call home has become an empty shell, a sad and distorted reflection of its former self. And it's hot! Don't think for a minute about jumping in the pool to cool off. No longer an oasis, the pool is now equal parts water and yard waste and has turned a stunning emerald green color. With no pump to move the water (no electricity, remember?), the pool is now a stagnant pond.

Even the kids are grossed out, and that's saying something. But, in the days to come, we would be very glad we had a pool, and do you know why? We had no running water. No, we didn't bathe in the nasty pool water; *we schlepped gallons of it into the house every time we needed to flush a toilet.*

Here is where I need to apologize to any Amish people who are reading this story as unlikely as that may be. I know that you lead very nice lives, albeit without electricity, and I don't mean to offend you by using your way of life as an analogy for a "dark" chapter in my life. I will make it up to you later, I promise.

We Floridians prepare for hurricane season every year by stocking up on batteries, flashlights, canned goods, water, propane, and first aid supplies-but we never really believe we'll need them. As a result, in this actual crisis, we were able to feed ourselves with no problem. Of course, with the refrigerator no longer refrigerating, there was a mad dash to cook and eat all the perishables before they actually perished. It took us much longer to prepare even simple meals, with no kitchen gadgets to help us and no microwave but, to our surprise, the food tasted delicious. Maybe it was the sense of adventure from cooking outdoors like cowboys on the range, or maybe it was the anticipation of waiting for the food, or maybe it was the fact that we ate together as a family with no interruptions and actually talked that made those meals so memorable.

With no work or school obligations the days were very long; we seemed to have stepped outside of regular time. Meal preparation and cleaning up afterwards took some time, but there was still so much of the day left to fill. For the first few days, the kids complained about missing their favorite TV shows. Knowing the shows are on and that you can't watch them is like hearing the fun party next door that you haven't been invited to. Okay, I admit it; I felt the same way.

After cleaning up the yard, we looked around for things to do. We read a lot and rediscovered that playing board games was fun, but it was hot inside, so we started spending more time outside. We took long walks and chatted leisurely with neighbors we hadn't seen in years, even though they lived in sight of our house. We listened to the battery-powered radio and talked to each other more, even though we spent some of that time whining. I was pretty whiny myself but, as the oldest member of the family, I had lived with comfort longer than any of them, so it was understandably harder for me...

Thirteen days later, when the power returned, we cheered. We kept the flashlights handy, just in case, but we didn't need them anymore. In no time, we returned to our old ways, watching TV, listening to music, talking on the phone, sitting in front of the computer, together but alone, entertaining ourselves with all of the luxuries electricity can provide. I never see the neighbors anymore because they are inside their houses doing all the same things we are. Sometimes, late at night, when everyone else is asleep, I spend some time in quiet reflection and I think... maybe it wouldn't be so bad to be Amish.

CRAZY HOBBIES

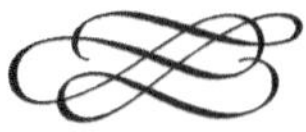

You think your childhood was normal, even now, *when you should know better*. The truth is that each family enjoys its own special brand of kookiness, including yours. Of course, I'm not talking about the people who end up on reality TV buried under all the stuff they couldn't bear to part with. I'm talking about people who keep the "fun" in dysfunctional, the ones whose little idiosyncrasies provide great stories at Thanksgiving.

In our family, we had a fondness for hobbies. Actually, *we* didn't, but our dad did. And it was much more than a fondness, it was more like an all-consuming mind-boggling eye-popping breathtaking overwhelming single-minded focus. But even with all that, he didn't forget about his children, no sir. We were all pulled into the vortex with him...

The first thing I remember is crouching down on our living room floor, immersed in a sea of coins, looking for rare pennies. In the beginning, my sisters and I had a great time rolling around in those thousands of pennies, throwing them at each other and cascading them from high in the air. But when our dad asked us to sift through them and separate them into groups according to their imprint dates, the fun was over. Now, before you start wondering if child services or the Labor Department had to get involved, let me just say-it wasn't like that. Far from running his own sweat shop, my dad wanted us to *love* coin-collecting. He gave each of us a penny collection book with empty slots for every year, including the rare pennies, and then tried to make a game out of it. And it might have worked too, if only we could have paced ourselves, but our dad only has one speed and that's full-speed ahead.

From pennies, he went on to nickels, dimes, quarters and JFK half-dollars. He started storing bags of coins in our closets for when we "had time to look through them" (they may still be there). He dragged us to coin shows and coin stores all over town. He bought necklaces made from rare coins and gave them to my mother for special occasions. She would smile and thank him and then put them away. She may have even worn them to humor him because, even though we were all tired of coin-collecting, nobody wanted to squelch my dad's enthusiasm. His quest for rare coins made him so happy. That is, until he discovered stamp-collecting.

Rather than bore you with the details, let's just say it was very much like coin-collecting only a lot easier to lug around. This time, he gave each of us a beginner's book for collecting stamps and we soon graduated to having our own individual country. For some reason, I chose the Vatican, although I can't imagine why. Their stamps weren't pretty, just a bunch of popes. And it's not even my religion...go figure.

While I don't remember the rest of the hobbies in chronological order, I do know that they went from small to large, from being contained in our basement to taking over our house and yard. There was jewelry-making, which was kind of fun for us because we didn't have to participate, and because we could always create a last-minute, unique birthday gift for a friend from the tons of beads, stones and materials my dad kept on hand. Then there was the "miniature" phase during which my dad furnished an entire miniature Victorian mansion from top to bottom (it was much nicer than our house), as well as assembled a miniature greenhouse with real plants in tiny pots. Ironically, it was the miniature greenhouse that led to my dad's most expansive, most labor-intensive and most annoying hobby of all: cactus.

I can almost hear them groaning as they read this, our friends and family who were dragged into the dangerous and dirty world of cactus. I don't mean to make it sound exciting, as if it involved espionage or working for the mob; it was *literally* dangerous and dirty.

After purchasing one small cactus garden at K-Mart, my dad went on to fill the entire back yard with every kind of cactus and succulent known to man, building two greenhouses to house them all. To this day, I cannot explain it. They were the ugliest plants I ever saw, even when they bloomed. And they were everywhere: every windowsill, every table and every empty spot in the yard. We could have lived with all of that (and, in fact, we did), if it hadn't been for the dreaded... *plant shows.*

Several times a year, plant enthusiasts gather at weekend plant shows, ostensibly to sell their wares but, in reality, to schmooze & steal each other's ideas. Not only was it unbearably hot (the shows were out-side, in Florida), but each show necessitated renting a truck and recruiting many helpers to gingerly pack up dozens of blood-thirsty cacti, knowing full well they would be packing them up again at the end of the show. This torture went on for years and only ended because my mother insisted they sell the house and move to a condo. I only hope the new owners never walked barefoot in the backyard...

Which brings me to the present, and the wacky world of metal chickens. Although he was sad about razing his greenhouses, my dad quickly recovered and started taking art lessons twice a week. After painting dozens of oil and acrylic landscapes, still life pictures, portraits and abstracts, he switched from painting canvas to painting metal art. Often using whimsical colors, he has painted hundreds of pieces including animals, insects, statutes of people, and some pieces that are so weird they defy description. My dad is quite prolific and generously donates many pieces to my favorite non-profit for their raffles. As a result, everyone I know owns a piece of Art (also my dad's name).

Now I know that my childhood wasn't typical, but, really, whose is? Although I often felt like the Karate Kid did when Mr. Miyagi gave him seemingly pointless chores, maybe I too learned something valuable. And while I don't have any crazy hobbies, I am enthusiastic about each task I undertake and give it all I've got. And for that, I guess I should say: "Thanks Dad!"

ASK ME NO QUESTIONS

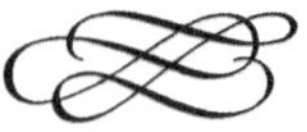

Now that I'm fifty, I actually long for the "good old days." No, it's not a false sense of nostalgia; I have a bona fide reason for feeling this way. There are way too many decisions to make these days. Even choosing a tube of toothpaste is exhausting. Gel or paste? Whitening or tartar-control? Prevent gingivitis or treat sensitive gums? It doesn't seem fair that I should have to sacrifice a dazzling smile in order to prevent tartar build-up. As if that would happen...

All of these choices are like Hydra's heads, if you remember your Greek mythology. Chop one head off and two more replace it, which brings me to the worst offender of all--the "Scale of Pain." No, it's not an in-strument of torture sitting next to the rack in the dun-geon, it's a tool embraced by medical personnel everywhere. You know the drill: as you writhe in pain, the doctor/nurse/technician looks concerned and asks you to "please rate your pain on a scale of one to ten." How can anyone answer that? If "one" is an annoying hang-nail and "ten" is screaming agony, how can we possibly assign values to numbers two through nine? I don't know about you, but my vocabulary just isn't nuanced enough to tackle this. Take a bee sting, for example. A sting on the toe might be a "5" but a sting on the lip would be, well I can't even assign a number to that. My dazzling smile would disappear altogether.

And, as if this task weren't already impossible, I often find myself using fractions! "The broken toe started out as a 4 and then crept up to a 4½ pretty quickly, but it was definitely a 7¾ by lunchtime ...." I am afraid my head may explode from overthinking this. And what number would I assign to that?

And speaking of numbers, let's talk about Mc-Donald's. They like really big numbers-"billions and billions". It's mind-boggling to think that with each hamburger sale, their hapless employees had to ask: "Would you like fries with that?" And, since "up-selling" worked so well for them, *everyone* is doing it now, to the point that I am barraged by non-stop questions and choices. The voice at the Starbucks drive-thru wants me to buy a breakfast sandwich and the voice at the bank drive-thru wants me to discuss their loan opportunities. My hairstylist tries to sell me expensive hair products and my vet pushes fancy dog food. Ads of all kinds pop up at every website I visit, all trying to sell me something. George Orwell predicted, in his prescient book 1984, that our very pillows would be flashing ads for us to buy toothpaste. I think we are there now; it just took us a bit longer to arrive.

But it's not all bad. After all, we are lucky to live in a wealthy country that can offer us choices. We know that our grocery shelves will always be stocked and we rarely have to wait in line, except at Disney World. I wouldn't want to live anywhere else and I am usually happy to be here, but, if you don't want to visit the "Scale of Pain," please don't ask me any more questions.

FRIENDS IN LOW PLACES

IT'S NOTHING PERSONAL, BUT I'M NOT FOND OF frogs. I think they're kind of ugly, although I try not to judge. For all I know, they think the same about me. Not that it matters, since we don't usually come into contact--what with me enjoying the comfort of my couch and them enjoying the comfort of wherever *they* like to watch "Dr. Who." But all that changed yesterday...

First, I should explain that I love to swim and by "swim" I mean splash around in my pool. Actually, I do much more than that but, if you saw me, you'd think I was just splashing around. Here's how it goes. Before I get in the pool, there is a crazy chatterbox in my head pitching fastballs into my brain, something like this:

How did it get to be so late? What can I make for

dinner? Are there leftovers? I need to order meds for the dog. Got to remember to buy stamps, milk, and... what was the third thing? I can't believe I forgot the third thing--I feel like Rick Perry! I am so losing it...

But, as soon as I wade into the pool, Ms. Chatterbox forgets all that and says, "Ahhh, this is nice!" If I'm lucky, I won't hear from her for the rest of the day. I then pick up the pool net and start circling the perimeter scooping up leaves and bugs (I can't risk getting a bug in my mouth. I'm sure you understand) while immersing myself oh-so-gradually. Once the pool is bug-free, I submerge and practice for my pretend audition with "Cirque du Soleil," underwater edition. I proceed to roll and tumble, pirouette and twirl--I just couldn't be more graceful. Of course, I can't see myself, so that helps.

After practicing my routine, I try to see how long I can swim on the bottom of the pool while scuttling like a crab. I imagine I look just like the blue crabs that sometimes find their way into our pool. And sometimes I simply free-float, swaying like a sea anemone and giving up control of my limbs. Control is overrated anyway.

But yesterday was different. As I was netting up the debris, I caught a glimpse of something moving. A tiny black frog, no bigger than a nickel, was trying to scale the slick tile wall of the pool and make his escape. I could see that it just wasn't happening for him. He was so cute and determined that I wanted to help. I offered him a lift on my index finger so I could ferry him out, but he had another idea. Grasping my finger with all his puny strength, he decided he liked it there and no amount of coaxing could convince him otherwise. I was touched. I couldn't help but smile as my little friend and I cleaned the pool together, basking in the afternoon sun. I lazily tried to remember anything I could about frogs and came up with only one thing: they love to eat mosquitos. I thought about how my friend's mother had contracted West Nile Virus, and how our dog had contracted heartworms even while taking preventative meds. Both of those were mosquito-borne diseases.

I suddenly realized that by saving my little frog's life, I might be saving a person's life! I was struck by how far-reaching one small act of kindness could be.

"I know you're nervous," I said, gently nudging him, "but it's time for you to go. You have a big job, you have to save the world!" He finally understood how important he was and reluctantly hopped away.

I've changed my mind about frogs, of course, how could I not? But I still won't be inviting them to watch "Dr. Who" with me on my couch.

MARTHA, I LET YOU DOWN

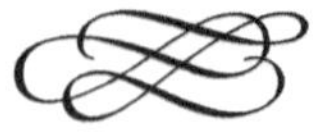

By no stretch of the imagination could you call me a perfectionist. I'm more like an "imperfectionist" in that I'd rather do several projects that are "good enough" than spend hours getting one thing just right. It's a system that works for me. But last night was an exception...

Every so often, the stars line up and I have a clean house, a well-manicured lawn and a well-stocked fridge all at the same time. It's a Martha Stewart moment for me and I relish it, walking around my house as it radiates with Feng Shui. I was in this Zen-like state last night when a disturbing thought shook me out of my reverie. We had nothing to eat. Oh sure, there were lots of ingredients, but nothing you could call a meal. As much as I hated to mess up my clean kitchen, I knew there was no way out of it, I had to cook--especially since our boys were home from college, they were always hungry.

Since I'd have to clean the kitchen anyway, I decided to make several dishes at once: a vegetable curry for dinner, mini corn muffins for breakfast, and a spinach quiche for whenever. I mixed the muffin ingredients together and spooned the batter into four muffin pans. While I waited for the oven to heat up, I defrosted the frozen spinach in the microwave and started chopping vegetables for the curry.

I have to clear something up at this point. Although my last name is "Venkataraman," you shouldn't assume that I'm Indian. The name came with the guy. And, while I have visited India, I didn't go there to take cooking lessons. Nevertheless, I do enjoy a good curry and can usually follow a recipe.

After I cleaned and chopped my vegetables and shoved all the peels, stems, etc. into the garbage disposal, I lined up my beautiful rainbow of onions, peppers, eggplant, cauliflower and potatoes. Just then, the oven beeped its readiness and I crammed all four muffin pans in at once. The muffins wouldn't take long and soon started to smell delicious. Our two dogs, Abby and Phoebe, were already camped out by the kitchen door, hoping for a sample. They were dreaming if they thought I was going to give them any.

As I heated the oil in the pan for my curry, I poured myself a glass of Merlot--I was sure Martha would've done the same. Then, following my recipe, I poured a tablespoon of mustard seeds into the hot oil and waited for them to pop. I didn't have to wait long before they started popping like popcorn and then hurtling themselves all over the kitchen! I felt hot oil pinging me everywhere at once. I tried to shove the pan to a back burner to make it stop (splashing hot oil in the process), but it was no use. The mini-grenades kept coming at me while I yelled, "Ow! Stop!" as if they cared. Just then, the timer went off for the muffins. Reluctantly, I put down the towel I'd been using to shield my face and sure enough, as I pulled out the first tray of muffins, a hot mustard seed flew into my eye--all the way from the back burner! The sudden shock made me drop the muffins which scattered all over the floor. That was all the invitation Abby and Phoebe needed. They raced into the kitchen like they were in the home stretch of the Kentucky Derby and started slurping up the hot muffins while covering the floor in dog slobber.

I was so busy yelling at the dogs that I didn't see the fire raging on the stove where I had spilled the oil. In a panic, I looked for the fire extinguisher. Was it under the sink or in the garage? The hot mustard seeds were still coming at me as I ducked under the sink. Grabbing the extinguisher, I pulled the pin and swung around, knocking over my glass of merlot and splashing it all over my shirt. After the fire was contained, I took the rest of the muffins out of the oven.

They were so burnt that even the dogs wouldn't eat them.

I took a deep breath. What would Martha do? She would try to salvage her shirt, I thought. I turned on the water in the sink to wet the sponge and water started to fill the sink. I flipped on the garbage disposal but, instead of the water draining out, food started shooting up! Apparently, I had overloaded the disposal. I turned off the disposal and walked over to the fridge. I knew there was a bottle of club soda in there somewhere. As I reached inside, I knocked it over. Not thinking, I opened the bottle and club soda sprayed everywhere, like a scene from The Three Stooges. Soaking wet, I sat down on the kitchen floor and started laughing. I heard the front door open and my oldest son came into the kitchen to ask, "What's for dinner, Mom?"

I shook my head as club soda dripped down my face. "We're ordering pizza."

I was sure that's what Martha would have done.

NO RIGHT ANSWER

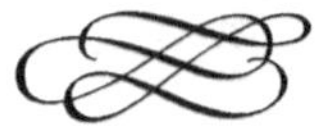

I decided to call my friend Melanie (not her real name) last week because I hadn't heard from her in a while.

"Hey," I said when she picked up, "How have you been?"

"Good, you?"

"Doing great," I said, "What's new?"

"Oh, not much."

"How's your family?"

"Everyone's good, thanks," she said.

I wondered why I wasn't getting much of a response from her as she was usually quite chatty. In fact, she seemed rather cool towards me. I racked my brain trying to think of what I might've done to deserve that. Finally, I just asked.

"Are you mad at me for some reason?"

"No, not mad."

"Okay...then, why do you sound mad?"

"Well, to be honest with you, I'm trying to be careful about what I say. I'm afraid you might write about me in one of your essays."

"What are you talking about?" I asked.

She sighed. "I know you were referring to me when you wrote about people who dote on their pets too much."

"No, I wasn't!" I protested.

"And," she went on, "You were definitely talking about me when you wrote about your friends with annoying food allergies."

"I swear that wasn't about you!"

"And when you wrote about people's phobias? Me, again."

"No, wrong," I interjected, "Did I even mention your phobias?"

"And the worst one was when you made an example out of my procrastinating. I'll never live that one down."

"But, Melanie, I wasn't writing about you at all, I was writing about me, my procrastinating!"

There was a long pause.

"I see," she said quietly.

"So, are we good?"

"Not really," she said stiffly.

"What's the problem now? I asked.
"Isn't it obvious? You think I'm too boring to write about."

WORDS OF WISDOM

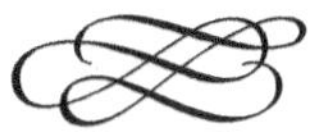

A FEW WEEKS BEFORE MY GRANDMOTHER, NANA Bert, died, she asked me to come see her. She was quite insistent-but then, she was quite insistent about most things. She was a strong and often abrasive personality, practically a force of nature. I must admit though, I was curious about why she had asked for me, out of all the grandkids. Did she have something to tell me? A family secret? A confession that I'd always been her favorite grandchild? How she'd managed to live to the age of 90?

I rushed over to her apartment and took a seat next to her bed and waited. She knew I was there, but she kept drifting in and out of sleep.

I prompted her. "Hi Nana, I'm here. How are you feeling? I heard you wanted to see me?"

She opened her eyes and said, "Barbara? Thanks for coming. I really need to talk to you …"

"That's what I heard, Nana. Well, here I am, what is it?"

She whispered, "I need you to…"

"Yes? Need me to do what, Nana?"

"I was hoping you could…"

"Could what?" I asked, gently.

"Could do something for me…" she murmured, half-asleep again.

The suspense was killing me. What could my grandmother possibly need from me that nobody else could do for her? I waited until she stirred again.

"Nana, what did you want to do?" I prodded.

She gave me a little smile. "I need you to finish cousin Betsy's afghan…can you do that for me?"

I sighed. "I'll try my best, Nana. You know, I'm not that great at crocheting. Is that all you needed to tell me?"

"Yes, thanks so much. I appreciate it."

I have to admit I was disappointed she didn't have some life lesson to impart or something important to say. On top of that, she'd given me a chore, and I do find crocheting to be a chore, since I don't know what I'm doing half the time.

It wasn't until a few years later, when I retold the story after a couple of glasses of wine that I realized those actually were words of wisdom.

My Nana was telling me: stay busy, finish what you start, do nice things for other people and ask for help when you need it.

And, now that I've told you, it's not a family secret anymore.

THE SWEET LIFE

MY MOM USED TO SAY I HAD "CANDY RADAR." SHE was right, of course, I do, but I can't take credit for it. I was born this way, it's my unique superpower. No other superhero can claim it--and I'm not sure they'd want to. No matter where I am, no matter what else is going on, I can always sense the presence of candy. I'm not kidding. Even if I was in a burning building, and a fireman threw me over his shoulder to carry me to safety, I'd be wailing: "Who's going back for the jar of jelly beans?"

It's not like I go looking for candy, you know. Well okay, I do, but most of the time it just appears in my line of vision, with no effort on my part. But, before you recommend a twelve step program for my sugar addiction, you need to hang on a sec. I said I had candy radar--I never said I ate all the candy I came across. Think of me more as a divining rod, a candy psychic as it were. I'm a Tootsie Pop cop, a Baby Ruth sleuth and a gumdrop gumshoe all rolled into one, ha ha.

That doesn't mean I don't eat candy. Au contraire! There's nothing like the burn of an Atomic Fireball rolling around your mouth, or the mouth-puckering sourness of a Lemonhead on the tip of your tongue. And nothing compares to the perfect piece of dark chocolate, melting like butter in your mouth and sending happy thoughts to your brain. Of course, I have gone overboard once or twice. I'm not proud of this, but I once ate a half pound of Jelly Bellies while working at the register in my college book store (you can't really call it an "impulse buy" if you've been eyeing it for three hours). But those days are over. My teeth and my waistline now insist on moderation.

Also, I need to set a good example for my kids. My oldest son doesn't care much for candy, but the younger one is another story. If I buy a pack a Sweet Tarts and stash it in my glove compartment, Josh will find it (and eat some). But it wasn't until the day that I took him to my office and he went straight for the dark office in the corner, opened the desk drawer and found a large bag of candy that had been placed there only hours before, that I knew. He had candy radar, too.

Perhaps one day the world will need people like

us for some higher purpose. After all, they can train pigs to sniff out truffles and they're even training dogs to sniff out cancer. Surely, they can use people who sniff out candy. I only hope they use our superpower for good and not evil!

IF I HAD TO CHOOSE…

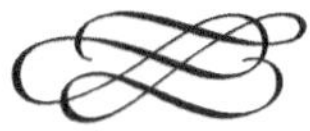

DECIDING WHICH INSECT I WOULD BE IS A daunting task, considering there are over 900,000 types of insects in the world, so I have narrowed it down to a few choices. One option is the cicada. Cicadas have been hibernating underground for seventeen years and are about to awaken to swarm by the billions. I would make a great cicada because I love to sleep and I'm very sociable-I would enjoy hanging out with billions of friends-but, then, I decided against it. There's way too much competition for everything AND, on top of that, cicadas are everyone's favorite meal. I'd have to spend all my time hiding from squirrels, birds, wasps and people. Besides, if I slept for 17 years, I'd never catch up on my favorite TV shows.

My next choice was an ant. It would be great to be an ant because they can lift 50 times their body weight. That would be like me lifting 7,500 pounds! My friends at the gym would be so impressed (if I actually went to the gym).But if I were an ant, my friends would be ants and they could all lift that much, so what's the point? Ants are really organized and believe in teamwork, but the life of an ant is just work, work, work, so I think I'll pass.

Bees are great, too--they really enjoy the outdoors and produce honey, one of my favorite things. But they're having a hard time lately with so many dying from "Colony Collapse Disorder," so I will have to pass again.

Being a butterfly is appealing because they get to live two lives, one as a caterpillar crawling around and then as a beautiful butterfly, but when I learned some butterflies only live a week, I knew it was time to rethink my decision.

When I read that termites have a soldier caste, I thought I'd found my favorite insect, but then I learned that they are usually blind and like to commit suicide, so that was definitely out.

Then I found my favorite insect, the cockroach: it's nocturnal, like I am; it can live anywhere, but prefers warm temperatures, like I do; it loves sugar, definitely me; and it's really hardy and who doesn't want to be hardy? I could be the insect everyone loves to hate. Although cockroaches and people have been locked in battle forever, we cockroaches know we're winning!

YOU THINK YOU KNOW A PERSON...

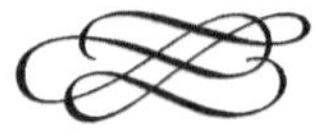

I JUST READ SOMETHING DISTURBING BUT, IF I tell you about it, then we'll both be disturbed. Remember--YOU HAVE BEEN WARNED.

Did you know that bacteria living in our bodies outnumber human cells 10 to 1?

10 to 1! That means, for each human cell in your body, there are ten microorganisms, which may include bacteria, fungi and archaea. I don't even know what archaea are--and I've read the definition! The only part I understood was that they produce methane, which stinks, both literally and metaphorically. In fact, the number of different bacteria species living on your skin alone could approach five hundred. And that's not just your skin we're talking about, it's mine too! And fungi! Do we have mushrooms growing out of our ears, or what?

And the news gets worse: each of us hosts thousands of types of bacteria with different body sites that have their own distinctive communities. For example, your belly button (an area I assume you never think about, unless you are one to contemplate your navel) can host any number of 1,400 strains of bacteria that call it home.

So, it turns out you can live in a gated community, but you can't be one. You have no say in the matter: you are a microbiome, an aggregate of microorganisms that live in your skin, your eyes, your mouth, your gut, and other places which I can't talk about in polite society.

Before you completely freak out, let me tell you that some of these organisms are beneficial, like gut bacteria that aid in digestion, and others that help maintain our health in different ways. The most unsettling news is that we have no idea what the majority of them do. But, have no fear, we (well, not me, of course, it's the 200 researchers in the Human Microbiome Project) are studying them in an effort to figure out what the little buggers are up to.

Of course, since they outnumber us 10 to 1, it seems that we ARE the little buggers!

A CASE OF AGE DISCRIMINATION

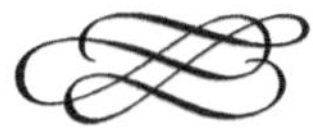

SHE AND I USED TO BE SO CLOSE, IT SEEMED LIKE we could read each other's thoughts. We knew all the same people, had the same hobbies, and enjoyed the same books--even our politics lined up. But that was before. When I saw her recently, she felt like a stranger. My first thought was, "Oh my God, you look so old!" I didn't say anything, of course, but she knew what I was thinking, it was all over my face. She looked so unhappy, too. I tried to smile and cheer her up, but she wasn't buying it.

Then, I decided to give her a pep talk about the good things in her life that had only come with the passage of time: the long friendships, the deep appreciation for nature, the poignancy of life itself. And how, when she was young, she couldn't understand the connectedness of everything, and how we are here for a higher purpose--to care for each other and lift each other up, to embrace a philosophy of loving kindness and compassion.

I explained that age isn't important at all, it's wisdom, knowledge and experience that matter. I really thought I was getting through to her, making her see what life was all about, but then she spoke.

She looked me right in the eye, those eyes with crow's feet imprinted on them, with an age spot on the left cheek, and said, "If you don't get me some Botox and a laser peel, sister, you'd better just cover all the mirrors in the house."

So I covered all the mirrors.

BITTERSWEET

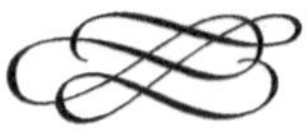

WHO WOULD HAVE THOUGHT THIS COULD HAPPEN to us? An economic superpower in our day and we never saw it coming. Okay, that last part isn't true. They did try to warn us: the botanists and economists, the climatologists and even those pretentious foodies, damn them! But we refused to believe it. So spoiled and gluttonous were we that we couldn't imagine such a vacuum in our lives, couldn't imagine that one of our greatest pleasures, second only to, well you know, could disappear so suddenly, leaving us in a glassy-eyed stupor.

At first, there seemed to be no cause for alarm. Sure, a few high-end distributors declared bankruptcy and most of the artisanal boutiques quietly closed down, but that didn't affect the rest of us. Even as the price started creeping up, we took it in stride, still happily gorging ourselves on a regular basis. Every holiday was an excuse to buy new varieties created in whimsical shapes or mixed with exotic flavors like hot chili peppers, spicy ginger, aromatic curry powders or edible flowers.

People even ate it on insects! Now, why would I make that up? Others drank it in liquid form; some preferred it melted or frozen. Touted for centuries as an energy-booster, an antioxidant, and an aphrodisiac, it was all that and much more. In fact, some of the wealthiest ladies went to luxury spas so they could bathe in it! Isn't that decadent? The flavors were so rich and complex that no scientist ever managed to synthesize it in the lab. Believe me, they tried. If I told you its name meant "food of the gods," maybe you could start to understand the depth of our loss...

In our defense, we had a lot of other problems to worry about. There were no world population councils back then so people could have as many children as they wanted. My own grandparents had twelve kids! The population climbed to 9 billion before we did anything about it. On top of that, the climate was changing and real estate which had been "underwater" due to the housing bubble was now literally underwater. Coastal areas were disappearing, Louisiana was sinking and the popular area known as South Beach was cut off from the mainland forever. At the same time, countries were locked in a massive power struggle over the dwindling supply of fossil fuels.

Is it any wonder we paid no attention to those whining foodies? I mean, they were always complaining about something. If it wasn't the shortage of truffle pigs, then it was the ban on pâté de foie gras or the counterfeit caviar flooding the market. Their concerns were so alien to the rest of us plebeians that we tuned them out when we really should have listened to them. Only the Doomsday freaks took them seriously and, naturally, they started hoarding the "food of the gods" because, well, hoarding was what they did best. Always preparing for the world to end, they saw no sense in going hungry while they waited. It was the hoarding that jacked the price up enough for the world to finally notice.

Outside of our purview, the fragile crops that supplied the delicious elixir were dying from insect infestation, disease, and climate change, and demand was quickly overtaking supply. Speculators entered the mix and real panic set in. It became the hottest commodity in the world, even overtaking gold. Financial markets were so volatile that in West African countries, where the crop was cultivated, ripe pods became the new currency, just like in ancient times. Black markets sprang up everywhere and nobody could talk about anything else. Elected officials were besieged by rabid voters demanding immediate action. Riots broke out and the processing factories were looted for raw materials. Even natural disasters couldn't distract people for very long...

I'm sorry, where was I? You'll have to forgive me but ever since I reached my 115th sun cycle, my mind has started to wander. Oh, yes, the governments became involved but, of course, they only made things worse. Truthfully, I don't know if there was anything they could have done anyway. Our best agri-scientists worked around the clock but, in the end, all they could do was bank seeds in all of the master seed banks and watch it play out. In only ten years, all of the crops were utterly decimated, never to return. Even the hoarders and black marketeers eventually reached their last precious morsels. And, because they had no choice, the people of the world adjusted, but there was a sadness that permeated everything, a yearning that would never pass, a taste that could not be forgotten...

I know you're wondering why I told you this long story, especially today, when we should be celebrating your 21st sun-cycle and eating a feast of the best synth food in town, but you're my only great-great-granddaughter and I wanted to give you something really special. Yesterday, I went to my Cryo-storage unit to get your gift so that it would thaw out in time. Here, please take this and remember to savor every bite: it's like nothing you've ever eaten before and nothing you will ever eat again. Yes, it is a curious shape, it's meant to resemble an animal that's now extinct; it was called a rabbit. I hope you don't mind if I watch you take a bite, it would give me great pleasure. Oh no, please don't cry! Like life, chocolate isn't meant to last. Only the joy of experiencing it lingers on.

NIGHTMARE AT THE SLEEP CLINIC

"Middle Age" may be a sneaky bastard, who deepens your crow's feet and makes you forget what you did yesterday, but his side-kick is far worse, and you never know where *he* will attack next. Will it be "cankles" or a muffin-top? A double chin or thunder thighs? You know who I mean. Yes, I'm talking about "Flab," whose very name inspires loathing and an irresistible urge to purchase exercise programs from infomercials. How can we be expected to fight this insidious villain? We try to suck in our guts, but he has *forces of nature* on his side, like gravity and inertia, and we are mere mortals.

With his warped sense of humor, he attacked me a few years ago, leaving me with the strangest flab of all: A FLABBY PALATE. No gym, no tiny barbells, no mini-treadmills could help me. You may wonder why this would be a problem; after all, who would see it? Not even I could see it and, believe me, I tried. But aesthetics aside, my flabby, lazy, no-good palate would stop my breathing dozens of times each night, leaving me gasping like a fish yanked from the fish tank. And, in the morning, I would feel like I had slept in the washing machine and not on the gentle cycle either. Strangely, my palate seemed to have no sense of self-preservation. *Didn't it realize that if I died because of its shenanigans, I was surely taking it with me?*

And so began my quest for a solution; in truth, winning *American Idol* would have been easier. On the recommendation of a neighbor who had been *cured* of his sleep apnea (also my diagnosis), I had a Pillar procedure. Tiny plastic rods were inserted in the roof of my mouth to stiffen it and teach that pesky palate who was boss. One of the rods popped out within a week, requiring more surgery and resulting in a lost day of work, not to mention a killer headache. Two thousand dollars later, I had succeeded only in reducing my bank account balance.

Next, my extensive research convinced me that daily vocal exercises, while simultaneously making weird faces, would do the trick. Unfortunately for the people in the adjacent cars (and I *do* apologize to *all* of you), driving time offered me the best opportunity to practice these bizarre moves. Although I probably avoided a lot of accidents doing these exercises (because people thought I was bonkers!), alas, I made no progress.

Desperation set in and I did what any rational person would have done in my position: I bought a didgeridoo through the internet and tried to teach myself to play it. In case this is your first encounter with a didgeridoo, it is a primitive, very large wind instrument, also known as a "drone pipe," invented by Australian Aborigines. Playing it properly necessitates mastery of "Circular Breathing," *breathing out while simultaneously breathing in*, a method scientifically proven to improve sleep apnea and, I am convinced, an excellent contender for "America's Funniest Home Videos." Watching hours of YouTube tutorials did nothing to improve my circular breathing "technique," and I use that word loosely. I sounded awful! If "drone pipe" evokes the sound of gently humming bees slurping delicious nectar from delicate flowers, then my playing sounded like a swarm of African Killer Bees angrily attacking a whoopee cushion. I stopped playing altogether after I hyperventilated during practice and dropped the didgeridoo on my antique dresser, cracking the glass top. We refer to this as "the didgeridoo incident."

Undaunted, I paid an oral surgeon to fit me for a "Snore Guard," ® a moldable plastic mouth guard that pushes the lower jaw out like an open cash register. The purpose of this curious device is to open up your airway. Making you look like a Neanderthal is just an added bonus. I could now sleep for a few hours at a time, but only on the living room sofa with my head propped at a 45 degree angle. I rarely kept the guard in all night because my sleeping self liked to toss it aside. Then, one morning, it was gone. I tore the room apart looking for it, certain that my dogs had eaten the most expensive piece of plastic in the universe, but no, my sofa was the culprit! The snore guard was jammed so deep inside that it could only be retrieved by slicing open the underbelly of the hungry couch. So, after yet more furniture destruction, I was still no closer to a solution. Not only was I exhausted, I had exhausted all of my options. Except for one, the one I had been dreading for two years, the one that involved torture, deprivation, humiliation, and missing my favorite TV shows. Just thinking about it gave me panic attacks and cold sweats but- what else could I do? I had to spend the night at... the sleep clinic!

I have never been experimented upon by aliens, but it can't be too different from a trip to the sleep clinic. Oh, they try to deceive you at first. A friendly technician leads you to a cozy bedroom while whispering encouraging words. She shows you the bathroom, tells you to relax and hands you a remote control for your television. *You will never see her again.* She is replaced by a grim, unsympathetic girl, impatient to start the torture who, without speaking a word, proceeds to attach dozens of wires all over your body, cinch belts around your rib cage and chest, affix a microphone to your throat and a monitor to your temples, squeeze an oxygen monitor onto your finger and, finally, put a mask on your face. Not just any mask, but a "Continuous Positive Airway Pressure" mask, CPAP for short. If you were ever unlucky enough to be caught in category 5 hurricane-force winds, and then those winds blew directly up your nose, you would know how a CPAP mask feels.

She finally speaks. "You need to go to sleep now," she says sternly and leaves. I try to give my most incredulous look to the camera, where they are watching me, but I can't move my face because of all the wires. Life has become surreal, Kafkaesque. I wriggle and squirm for the next two hours like a bug under a microscope. Just when I think my stress level can't go any higher, a scolding voice over the intercom warns me that if I don't go to sleep, I will have to come back and repeat the study! Despite everything, I somehow, finally, fall asleep, only to be awakened minutes later by my nemesis. "One of your wires fell off," she mutters, as she roughly reattaches it. Then the squirming and scolding cycle resumes until 5:00 a.m. when I am unceremoniously unwired disconnected and told I must go home. As if I wanted to stay!

After two years of dreading it, my nightmare at the sleep clinic was over. Usually, fear of the unknown seems laughable in the end and so, in that light, I offer you this advice about the sleep clinic-RUN! SAVE YOURSELF, DON'T LET THEM GET YOU, TOO! Just kidding, not really...

Now I use a CPAP machine to unleash gale-force winds nightly against my flabby palate, which has stopped trying to kill us both. Although the mask makes me look like Darth Vader, and sound like him too, it's not *that* terrible. I imagine that, one day, I will embrace (not literally, that would be weird!) my CPAP machine for the life-saver it is- but it won't be today. And probably not tomorrow either.

Dear reader,

We hope you enjoyed reading *Quirky Essays For Quirky People*. Please take a moment to leave a review, even if it's a short one. Your opinion is important to us.

Discover more books by Barbara Venkataraman at https://www.nextchapter.pub/authors/barbara-venkataraman

Want to know when one of our books is free or discounted? Join the newsletter at http://eepurl.com/bqqB3H

Best regards,
Barbara Venkataraman and the Next Chapter Team

ABOUT THE AUTHOR

Award-winning author Barbara Venkataraman is an attorney in South Florida where she draws inspiration for her books from the daily headlines. She loves connecting with readers through her books and finds a particular kind of joy in a well-turned phrase. In addition to writing fiction, she co-authored *Accidental Activist: Justice for the Groveland Four* with her son Josh Venkataraman about his successful four-year quest to obtain posthumous pardons for The Groveland Four.

Quirky Essays For Quirky People
ISBN: 978-4-86752-400-8
Large Print

Published by
Next Chapter
1-60-20 Minami-Otsuka
170-0005 Toshima-Ku, Tokyo
+818035793528

29th July 2021